—————

DEMO

—————

ALSO BY CHARLIE SMITH

Poems

Jump Soul: New and Selected Poems
Word Comix
Women of America
Heroin and Other Poems
Before and After
The Palms
Indistinguishable from the Darkness
Red Roads

Novels

Ginny Gall
Men in Miami Hotels
Three Delays
Cheap Ticket to Heaven
Chimney Rock
The Lives of the Dead
*Tinian**
*Storyville**
Shine Hawk
Canaan
*Crystal River**

*published in a collected edition entitled *Crystal River*

DEMO

POEMS

Charlie Smith

W. W. NORTON & COMPANY
Independent Publishers Since 1923

To Arlo Haskell

CONTENTS

ACKNOWLEDGMENTS

Tin House, poetry.org, American Poetry Review, Ploughshares, the New York Review of Books, Plume, Poetry, Kenyon Review, Crazyhorse, Rattle, Southern Poetry Review, Southwest Review, American Journal of Poetry, Five Points

To the editors and staff of the magazines that first published many of these poems, my thanks

DEMO

NIGHT ALL DAY

Here, Dog

You say dogs
prefer the smell of the people they love
        and say everyone, even whole groups, according
to what they eat
and how they are arranged, emit a typical smell
        their dogs can recognize, and the way they look contributes to this
and how they move like ponies
crashing through bamboo
        or crushed souls fleeing midnight rooms, and rarely do dogs
if ever get mixed up
about this,
        they're always on the lookout as night
enters the ancient streets
without signs or balustrades wound
        with roses, and you say the dogs are here, standing stiff-legged
by the hedge or writhing in happiness,
and you, sweating,
        or stinking of an angry lover's perfume, are recognizable
and taken in, a wanderer
troubled or excised from the rolls,
        resentful, or nervous about money, the dog has put you
under his wing
and hurries you into the familiar estancia
with a love that can't be lost
        or beaten out of him as it has been lost and beaten out of you.

This Water Tastes of Iron

My tattoos tell love's story in miniature, which I prefer.
My dips in style, the picture I painted on a pool cover,
express a reckless calm, unsubstantiated but plush.
I pray to the ticking sound I hear at night. Breezes,
shaped in Africa, remind me of friends
buried in the sea. For years I lived in a home for the blind,
working the semaphore. My over-obvious
rectitude bought only time. Let's drain
the dark, she said, from every room. The mottos
on the radio scratch lately at my door, unverifiable
and hilarious. The past sinks like a body in a well.
I read the Bible for the stakeouts and descriptions of terrain.

Why Harp on It

In the stillness of dawn when the air hangs back and you plunge your hand
into the bottomless dark of a jasmine
bush when roosters crack the day open under a slurry sky and you've
forgotten why you're awake
and don't know why you're thinking of the time you gave the go ahead
for your mother's shock treatments and she came out
blank and ironical unable to squeeze orange juice and you poured her a drink
and she said Thank you I am very tired
and you were moving to Sioux City and didn't have time to say good-bye
and for a couple of years lived in a motel
and ate Chinese-Mex and supported a young car hop who needed
the money for her rattled
child and you'd wake at dawn with your deepest bones
aching like you'd gotten old before your time and there was no way
to be sure of anything and red gazelles
goff's pocket gophers atlas bears heath hens blue walleyes thicktail chubs
sea minks dire wolves catahoula
salamanders and xerces blue butterflies were already gone from the earth.

Crostatas

in rome I got down among the weeds and tiny perfumed
flowers like eyeballs dabbed in blood and the big ruins
said do it my way pal while starlings
kept offering show biz solutions and well the vatican
pursued its interests the palm trees like singular affidavits
the wind succinct and the mountains painted blue
just before dawn accelerated at the last point
of departure before the big illuminated structures
dug up from the basement got going and I ate crostatas
for breakfast and on the terrace chatted
with the clay-faced old man next door and said I was
after a woman who'd left me years ago and he said lord aren't we all.

This Right Here

In restricted access, in lockdowns,
with a price on the goods, the particulars
        shrouded, wearing trash cans for boots, the spring,
that won't testify, the cunning
like a worm in the guts of its own stupidity, braced against the seawall,
the spring, and why would I say this, or better,
let me tell you about the wildwood, that slumped masterpiece
        tick infested teeming with bugs,
the stinking ocean sloshing onto the rusticated shore,
you notice this in springtime like a calculation
continually misfiring, like a scrap of paper left on the table
explaining the shootout, the dishonor at dawn,
        and something bangs against me, I am overmatched
by a morning with rain, by the compressors
the catafalques groaning, you say it's springtime
and the birds, troubled with psychosis,
their wings stained with creosote, press northward,
        compelled by a remarkable idiocy, uninvented,
hauling their bodies through the standard acidity
and friendlessness into dune shadows
like the breath of satire, it's springtime
and runners are expected from the gravediggers
        with an appeal for more shovels, and the vines
crawl like murdered drunks
crawling in the dreams of their children, fiddling with the locks.

Samsara

The ocean, uncomfortable with itself, bangs and slurs,
mixing flavors, holding its own against infinity, scarred with ice. I rummage
in the window planter, arrange purslane and sundew to catch
the fairskinned day's best looks; the sun, winter's ear bob, hangs in a blue left to fade.

I'm going home, sings the celebrated pianist downstairs, a man of Africa,
traveled ages to sit before the #2 Concerto in A Minor. In my dream, cabbage roses
offered by my former wife, who stood wrapped in a red navajo blanket
by the doorway of an old hogan on the rez, shone. She's gone now,

into the far lands of chaos; sun-shaped molecules, scent of sweet bay,
figurations of reordered atoms I'll never recognize without a guide, all that's left.
These dreams let me know we're still together,
dancing before headlamps on the beach, or converting

our savings bonds to cash for a run to Old Mexico. The sun swings along,
carrying an old silver pocketbook—or that's the moon,
jaunty, not so pushy really, only too happy to forget the night. Plum flowers
and the first pear blossoms, all the white concatenations gather

at the bottom of the yard. The wind picks up speed,
remembering its days in Paris, in Ihpetonga and Tobruk. Conversions
at this latitude are frequent, but rarely sustained; the old ways
were more comfortable, the pies and Franco-American customs, dollops

of pure cane syrup on biscuits, the rye grass streaked by an invisible hand,
still pretty irresistible. I've caught up lately on everything
but time. An old leak, faintly corrosive, smelling of
uncleaned butter churns, whistles as it goes by, not minding much of anything.

AUGUST RAIN

Lacquered Dead

Balled-up clouds above the graveyard dab the shine off stars.
The dead fume up, spurious and superior, exchanging
love's gaudy reasons for a sub-section replacement
of elementary particles. Like you I'm a dying tribe. What I know
shines a moment—like leaves the cat licks—then returns to its place in line.
Get ready, the prophet says, but overlooks the dream-stalked,
the solitaries rowing the Straits of San Juan, loose flubbers
out walking the pinched streets of Fez. A taw-eyed woman on the edge
of madness leans from an upper story, catching all of space in one goggled glance.
Queer blue sky smeared with zinc. Each of us bent into one of the shapes
God makes. Fudged by will. Foot bones, casters, melon rinds—
emptiness, the future—wash in the runoff. Living's the least of it.

(Adirondack)

Something's falling in increments of banging and slight popping, klunks,
and then little
chittering rolls,
the roof I mean is being hit by objects
nuts, fruits
of the season: this miserable natural world
hurls these things . . . and then there're the wolf howls
or coyotes
as they call
them here and the barks and snuffles of so-called bears
and yesterday I saw a small tub-bottomed bishop
crossing the road on all fours—porcupine,
they said—and crows
strut
and there are these mincing deer so theatrically bold
and turkeys like drab bloated chickens
and tiny
bronze frogs
singing in my shoes
and last night as in the car I huddled over a radio broadcast
the stars lit up
in uncanny
formations: bright pegs
pictures of my tormentors and ex-wives . . . seemed to hang from:
and I showed them the frogs: shiny as coins of the caesars.

Sob Story

. . . actual tottering that takes place late
in the season, the recently
capsized trees, lindens arranged so they protect
the settlements

the cities, the oaks slowly giving in to
paralysis
the uncultivated elms
never touched in certain places

the cumbersome loosely arranged willows
down by the pond
illusions sputtering,
it's time for the weather report

that haunts us like
a death certificate, the icteritious following
like tiny rabbits
blowing everything on lunch,

a tidiness in the faltering
clouds we've seen before,
longing
calling a substitute to take over

the last bit of wallowing
we'll recall on closed up nights
when the stars
like spittle stuck to your shirt

beckon in what looks like a new way, speaking
in a new way of dust
and alarms
playing tunes you remember from childhood.

INVENTED DESTINIES

Volto

A spacial infirmity, what's closed-up like a child in a closet,
calls too softly to be heard. Like the little stream
with the broken back, that behind the barn collects
the bitter run-off. A specialized sky foretells the fall
of humankind. Clouds like saggy diasporas.
The fields flex their big muscles, getting ready for the stare-down
with the stars. It's winter, then summer comes
perfumed with toiletries. Raspberries bend quadrate
branches, the fruit like children about to swing into eternity.
I'm limited, she says, *but not alarmed, and ineffectively violent.*
Sometimes we block love like dump trucks on strike at the kiln.
The closed-off future taps at the window. It's the echo
that's scary. Suffering completes its tax return,
listing no dependents. The papered-over bits have shifted in the night.
Grim looks grimness in the eye. The dead taste of salt.
At the site tiny storms rage among the balled-up dresses.
Someone's heart's split open and used for a mask.
Sounds like love, says the mayor, *but then to me everything does.*

Cash Flow

Since you asked, yes,
the hotel is still down the street and the persistence
in capsule form of illusion pertaining to one's standing
in the order of development is, not astounding
exactly, but fraught with the scent of scholarship
and devilment, a casual glance
in itself enough to place you inside the scout hut
at the time of the murder, the joshing
and rib tickling shenanigans of those confined
by the govt for inexplicable acts always out there
just ahead of the dogs, the basic premise lost among weeds
by the river like the time we struck out
for the mountains on rumors of gold, the big mules
loaded down with equipment
and someone up ahead singing a song about
love's fits and smashups, the way we told ourselves
there'd be another chance, the grandeur we always depended on,
and beauty, they said, our true love, like a reference
to small time game preserves where the operators
herded the animals into thickets
and far fields the customers could never find
and there set up tents and offered free vittles
as if the arrangement met some kind of standard theretofore
unpracticed in the country where most
were only the tarnished trophies of those for whom the get-go
was just another way of saying the doctor is not in.

Wilderness

rain like drops of cold lead—
it's hard in this city to keep a grip on the natural world
poking its snout through the wovenwire fence on 7th
or while ordering fried chicken to go on Ave C
where once the carts like tiny sailing ships brought
alarm clocks and unblessed remnants the linden leaves
and locust leaves like green insertions blow
down 5th to meet the stiff leaves of bur oaks
and elm leaves like slender jimmies for all the locks
of memory on 8th—the remains of a garden
or lost civilization rise to a grassy mound where
children veer into fantasy and only bits of spotless sky
torn from a secret book appear above the lost and broken.

WHAT I DON'T KNOW

From Heine

Wo wird einst des Wandermüden . . .

Where will I lie in the bye and bye
where will I lie?
In fresh snow under northern lights
permafrosted in a stony field?
In a desert hole
of mixed borax and sandstone dust?
With a few dozen others tossed
in a pit after a friendly fire massacree?
Or slumped untended
on a weary slog from one unsuitable
home to the next
ex-animate and overlooked?
Anyhow, the whole policky skittish harangue
of comets and skirly
planet types space dust and infinite
jitters will surround me, lamps of a looted paradise.

One Spell

Now these redbirds,
cowbirds, flickers making
noise in the boxwoods, jasmine
trellis, thrushes and vireos
clambering in the straw, poking
out the eyes of children,
and bugs, waxwings, catbirds in
wax myrtle bushes, yaupons,
heart-wing sorrel plants in
cutover fields, warbler and oven
bird saying *teach-er, teach-er,*
nobody showing up for months,
mother drunk under the vines,
redstart and bobolink, lover
of hayfields and grasslands,
oriole hardly ever away
from the nest, mass migrations
of blackbirds and other seed eaters,
songbirds, all gone from here.

The Casing

For years I sat in bars lying about everything,
concealing my limp, offering vinyl
suitcases for sale and proposing to women
who'd overlooked themselves. I gave away

folding tables and threatened
species like lopsided turtles and misused
harness bulls. I wasn't as speedy as I claimed to be
or as galled by those without

a purpose in life. I sold three-day
vacations to resorts that existed
only in my mind. I liked to watch the breeze
take leafy boughs in hand.

The limits to man's ability
to reach the stars were no problem for me.
I sank my nose in foreign papers
looking for tiny lots I might build

my dream house on. I said I owned
hotels and racks for smoking arctic char.
I claimed to notice something burning
in the kitchen. A leaf seemed at times to urge

a change in plans. Probably the winds
were coming from the other quadrant. I gave away
my watch and told the time by the degradation
of building materials. I spelled the stuporized.

The sun, an old friend, eased
onto the brickyard wall. I sensed an era
drawing to a close. Something told me,
so I said, to gather my things. Smoothed-

over ideas, frets, a capacity for change
unremarked by others, a boarding house
menu I used for a text, my bindle, palpebral musings,
a burial suit of lights

and a jar of brandied apricots—all these
I said I'd send a van back for and never did.

No Nonsense

split off for a sec
I thought I might say something
truthful
but couldn't come up with it
and lingered in the rosy twilight
unpacking an old suitcase
I found under the stairs

sometimes I stay as still
as possible and tell myself
a limitless vista's
opening up when it's not

the rain pounded madly on the roof

afterwards we
sat on the porch shelling
peas and quoting scripture

the birds in the melaleuca trees
seemed tired

the sky
reopened like a grocery store
on a desert road

I came
away from myself
unstuck

and a sort of translucent
orderliness
like a small herd of gazelles
entered my mind

RAW EARTH

The Layout

Morning, knocked off the blocks, de-amplified
and clamped to daylight, the forests showing off their skinny bones

and the winterized animals brisk and shoveling messy leavings
down their gullets, the brandished bits in your mind like a vacation

in the tropics where at the cathedral the inventor of equipoise
loses his balance and falls flat. The damage is done. Carpenters

and light-fingered apprentices on their way to the arena, the careful
planning that's supposed to make the lamps come on at the sound

of eagles screaming, these placements detailing frostbite
in the mountains might mean we'll be back in the loggias

and fruit stands of our youth, someday. The gimmies, the shucked
superlatives like hosed-down relatives, the way she got on with it

after the tragedy, these secernate jump starts—
we get out early most days, wreathed in spumescence,

the basic compilations of a destiny transformed as we speak
into a vagueness of aspect like a murky rinderpest and invitation

to a crab boil on the beach. We escaped easily
the attitudinal ambiguities and hooted from the porch

at the passing armies. Bravery is after all a known quantity.
The getalong ways, conversationalists offering their cut rates

and specialized phrasing, the details of the fire traced with a blackened
finger on a placemat. It gets impractical you might say to go on.

Ithika

private disputes in the sweet apple
trees and a certitude

attested to by loquats and the hard-shell baptist
spiders

collecting rents

the way you look at me after you knock me
silly with kisses

and what's up with the elementals I say
the dog

lurks in the cabana like Ulysses
shadowing his old lady

the calculations
          fixing the tide

and *the inexpressible* surrounding the fort
these particulars

left over
when we boiled the affidavits

add up
to the spitting image

of true north
she says

covering her left eye with the hand
holding the deed

to the trailer
and a crushed floral tribute

and suppose—she says—
my typical effervescence was replaced

by an obscurity
heretofore unmentioned in the ranks

and the fake
voyage

turnd out
to be the voyage.

Stuff Your Cries into the Hamper and Hitch Up

Where the grass touches me I tremble
and phone Sister Mary Celeste
who's breaking the hearts of weeds in a garden
like a battlefield, who says
"This modification, these tremors, my cross-eyed soul—
You get me, don't you?"—and pretends
trucks are carrying her victuals away
and hangs up. This morning I woke to rain

spattered on the screen and silence along the rooftops
where on clear days you hear the starlings
preparing themselves for the inevitable. In the park
weeds writhe,
bolting already, and women,
clarified and promising themselves they'll not be misled,
plus hawks, cranks, the fretful men at the edges
scared they'll be picked off, the absolute courage

of anyone who hangs on until the end,
all add up, the point blank cavalcade you might say,
and pick up
where you left off last year, humming
or cursing under your breath, the small time gangsters of rectification
chipping away at their cells, the scars
right under your feet that the dust pats back into place,
proof of an ongoing perfection, and it's been like this all day.

ASSISTED LIVING

September Flowers

we grow slightly tired of the reconstructive
lantana circles benday dots
and raster of echinacea daisies crowding the scene
dwarf maples
waving their brown used
tissues and the silver grasses that keep on fiddling
with the wind and the crepe
myrtles check their weapons at the door
and goldenrod and mocking asters
quiver slightly
and the soft-hearted
birches still climbing the mountain
of their interest
issue statements that so far
mean little and the morning glories
roll their soft blue
hips and the telltale secretly
crushed
hearts of loosestrife lobelia and hosta
dash off
letters they'll never send
and gladiolus speak frankly to the breeze
about what it means to be
alive and hushed up
in the dark and in the september crowd
get lost as fall sinks the last cuts
in summer's fancy
life in cool water like a suicide
going down for the count.

Permission to Emigrate

The light leans gracefully into oaks and whatever was about to stop: stops.
But nothing does. The whole rheotropism pushes
on as if that's just fine, perfect, the explanatory
events canceled probably . . .
though this isn't bad . . . and the little variances
in which we stay a while in Yuma or Santa Fe . . . important to everyone, you notice,
not us . . .
the soft mornings
when we wake from an old bony sleep and wander around thinking of the great odes—
all this replicated in moments when the agony lets up
temporarily and whoever that was at the door
stops knocking and . . . you can tell . . .
just stands there . . .
maybe thinking of a girl in Omaha. How would we know? This the secret
of course:
the mind,
if it's the mind, refreshed by interception
of the composed and quickening universe . . . possible yet:
streets of Laredo, you say . . . and a feeling of plenty, like someone cornered . . .
still kind.
And so you go
on, like Schopenhauer,
temporarily free of indigestible self concern,
ratty cravings and such. Though nothing's being gathered . . . really . . .
or put aside. We're making it up: and using it as we go.

On the Whole

forced labor by now it seems for
ratty flowers, the few
wobbly
bees still at it, birches,
thinly dressed
myrtles, a wiry plant
tricked out in tiny
blooms
like red tear drops,
the whole outfit
stuck
with it,
every space shuttered,
self
untethered
gasping,
curdled yellow leaves
on the lawn,
each separation and elementary
episode
only a new version
of the same
ensemble, so
they say, but what about
these flowers, bristles, soft
pinks of mimosa,
gold crowns scattered in the lantana,
time, etc.,
not sleepy,

but enflamed at the edge of the hill,
glaring
as the sun carries
its red dog home.

Slumberland

down in slumberland the coldly available cattle bosses
get together, like the staff in a cheap hotel

for travelers blown in off the rainy desert says the old timer,
the blast of wind pounding the backs of downbeat ladies

and gents each with his own dead bird smell,
the drainage a little off, thin tubes taped to their sides,

the bosses offering no explanation of why after living in this world without
a single desire to leave the scene we are thrown one day

into a box and shoveled into the swampy dark
to lie with dirt in our mouths for eternity says the old timer,

pulling a pistol-shaped lighter
from his coat made of bulldog hair. it's slumberland out in the sticks,

the bill of cunning manufacture's arrived, the astonishing
complicity with almost everything to hold on he says,

to the last breath, like small
town waiters with greasy hands who never returned your change,

even sadness faltering, the ring fingers of old women
deeply gouged . . .

TRAMWAY

Genuine Risk

Troubles like a set of webbed yellow duck feet
in the Chinese butcher shop,

emails printed out from my old lover
speaking of life in the coalfields, heaps of char

and chunks of substance everything useful's extracted from—
like what we were up to, she says,

nothing left at the end but piles of gray pocked
matter in brown rainwater puddles,

this way I have about now, I say,
of remembering the worn out flopped over

daffodils in soaked mountain fields
and the heavy bodies of old draft horses,

the bunched uselessness of their muscles
as they stand in the impound

awaiting slaughter, in these circumstances you can bring up
almost anything, she says, the badgering,

the infirmities of your parents,
the old man yelling

with a panicked, penetrating feebleness
as the sky darkened

under the coming cyclone, I say, and the palm fronds
clattering and shaking suddenly hard

as a woman will shake her long wet hair, she says,
disturbed and hating the argument,

the cold quiet sureness
after that when there's a flatness in her eyes

as she looks at you
and you know nothing can be the same again, I say.

Backseat in Kinshasa

a crisis averted in gulfport pops up again in forest hills
or someone's talking about a job bucking timber or after a cold
lobster supper on the cape its fabricator forgets the singular phrase
that explains everything and then you're revoking
yesterday's permit or tailing a cheat across lower manhattan
or you've just changed the name of your dreamboat and it's time
for your pills or it's time for a check-in with the vastness
and the preacher is crying over the dappled gray running last
in the fourth at pimlico and the bomb removal squad is just leaving
your apartment or you are unable to drop the loose talk outside
filene's basement or spring is nowhere near this town
and the operators all reach home at the same time and you understand
everything means something else and weren't told that cabbage roses
went out of style or the proceeds from the caper long ago were lost

No Claim

A tense obligato, the light comes up out of a shallow grave.
It was only resting. Sulphur butterflies, taking a holiday
in the garden, one in shades of yellow and orange, the other
the same plus chestnut spots, drift above
white-faced mallows, giving a sense of softness, richness
to the situation, paralleling the stinks and murder
poking up everywhere, each an elaboration of presence, minus
idea and will, the soul, we think, something like this,
gliding through the somatological world, airy, when maybe it's not,
maybe just an overweight bumbler, clumsy sporting-goods salesman
of the spirit, slumped by the road in a used Eldorado with
the window down, sweating in the dog-day heat, one we pass
irritably, exhumaceously by, as we hurry to the rendezvous.

FLEURETTE AMERICAINE

Issues with a Right-Hand Turn

Sometimes I'm issued a new head
and the old one drops
off and then I see the new one isn't new
it's a used
head, sometimes a bit moldy
or flushed
with rage, this head
filled with notes on what is wrong with the world
or carrying a list
of expendables or groceries
a head that remembers sunset casting
a golden shine
into the wheat
or the painting of a pig on a dinner plate,
or once I got
a head filled with memories
of snowy nights
when she dared me to love her, but I couldn't
speak the part
and had to set this head down
beside the road
and go on for the rest of that episode
headless, heedless,
one you couldn't hang for his crimes
if you wanted to.

This Far'll Do

the coast along here smells
like a rusty washing
machine still
in use. the sudsy
clouds are in on this. the sharks and flounders
know what's going on.
old plaques and busted dance floors
teeter among brushy
trash. discolored boilers filled with
bullet holes rest
like blue whales in the spit-
colored sand.
you can't walk ten feet
without
having to crawl over something.
skate eggs
shrivel in gray
sunlight. slithers of sea lettuce rot.
the meaning
of the world is in plain sight.
crabs line up
to turn themselves in. three hots
and a cot would do fine.
redfish belch
and puke up supper. the fix
is in—everybody
knows this.
we're beyond catastrophe
says the cod.
you could go on forever, but why bother.

Official Document

I was broke for a decade,
hummed, startled relatives with supposedly
official requests
for relief, cozened, elaborated
in company
on zany forecourts, the blaring sun
mashing the heart out
like a stogie, ran a small concession
selling popcorn
and ginger snaps, the waste
all around us I said
my mind
wandering to the greenish bend
in a sump stream
and supple, equivocating light,
the most dangerous
not so bad after all, I suctioned up
bits of spiritual
nonsense, pressed
complications, and listened to an old man
lie about his life,
a wry, intemperate sensation
overtaking us both.

SHORE LEAVE

Rush Shoes and Escapes

in the book about trees
a few
urban
derelicts buckthorn
ailanthus
the dependable honey
locust are all
I think about
some days the rain of blossoms
in summer
you get the picture
about the universe needing
plenty
of space the rapid thoughts
of an unarmed
man
the spot near the old water wheel
a day so cumbersome
it can't be raised
on the telephone the moment
you come back
to yourself as if from the stars

Still, Life

hydrangeas drained of color the forwarded rectitude of last roses
brained by fall the comfortless moment when the dog
stands staring at the silence trapped in a syringa bush we get so
we are almost free of elegance or a sense of the lostness
of everything the wild scramble held tightly by force the planet
turning rust red you can smell us all the way into space
the boys vomiting into buckets the girls unwrapping toiletries
we place ourselves in line with the sun the ancient cries drifting
 across the lake at dusk must mean something but we don't know what

Stroke

In the latest web of branches,
cuddled and
softened by a clandestine wind, before a sky clotted
and gauged and calling home to mama
who's dead, the taste of oranges in your mouth,
a moment when you stand
helpless before all you know about
yourself, a soft voice speaks. *Shake that back end, buddy.*
Meanwhile the tiny propellers of antique
aircraft turn. You smell the bony
dust in
the prairie grass. Sometimes your favorite
color changes
to aqua. *Everything's*
collapsible, the guy next to you on the subway
platform says. You're up
for the Simple Simon
part, a precision
unknown in your circle. Galvanized
washtubs stacked
in front of the funeral home. *Parts,* a woman sez.
A child at the curb works out his route
to fortune.
The cities at the corners of the map
are beginning to droop.
We remember how funny that was
the first time.

Wyoming

trees backed off
from basic training, stumped bracken, little to report

from arterial trenches
                landslides in the next county

water sources
that need looking after

old men oil their weapons
        then lose track of what they had in mind

it's all right
most days I look at the same calendar

scene of purposeful forgetting
            local incidents of disrepute

hard fists of balled grass
remnants of great disputes among the cottonwoods

the underrated collections
        of deertongue and switchgrass

nothing here
built for comfort

old cultures dribbled out to gray dreams
           at dawn and fogs reeking of tar.

Shop Blues

pigeon-eating
hawks green mire the dead
retriever dumped
in the public
trash
can
the desolation of a wild night
of storms
the softening of
the brain
after too much
worry you
said we are the ancients
wandering empty halls
the shattered
brilliants and costly receipts we pass
between
us no help—tiny island chains
of faith
swamped—a small bucket of leftover
shrimp
attracts rats
leptospirosis
lymphocytic choriomeningitis
plague
dropping one tall gent
another testy blonde with a lisp
four sales personnel
in their tracks

RAISE THE DEAD

Bolt Upright

home from work my father
would throw himself face down writhing
on the old couch as if he was smothering a fire
his body raw
from the chemicals at the plant
his wrists revealing the cords he was stretched by
that pulled him into
jaundiced shapes
and left him spinning in fumes
the disaster of his life that he endured
without mentioning
it even to my mother who
fixed elaborate suppers from a book she found
at the library
and never returned
at the table they would hunch shamefaced
over their food
like the early primates
who knew nothing of the world
outside the woods
no sense of broadway or of rooms filled
with paintings scattering the beauty of life before them
not even a religion
or a hope only us children
they lifted their battered heads
and stared at as if
we were creatures just called back from the dead
that they did not remember.

Belfast

I woke up still trying to understand things
and something about the moist smells of early morning
the collapsible flowers
pretending everything's all right
really got to me as if I was a monk standing in a dry river bed
trying to recall what the world was like
before he left it, and I drove to the supermarket
and got a bucket of chicken and thought about Rachel
who's probably driving home from work now
in Belfast, maybe talking as she drives to the handsome detective
she's dating, and sometimes I think of lakes, clear and taut
after the wind dies, of how voices travel far over them
unhindered at dusk no matter what you are saying.

Counting on My Fingers

snow day for the soul she says
and pulls out her list of plants that thrive in winter
hemlock pines firs
shimmying in sunlight evergreen
live oaks ilex
laurel and camellias boxwood holly
the stiff drapes
of mahonia represented
as colorful on snowy days when trains
pant lonely on
suburban tracks and the old men
press their faces
against loved ones like representatives
of a culture
that could kill you easily juniper
and daphne she says aucuba the streaked stiff leaves
of moonshadow
hemlock cedar on the path
down to the beach where a girl was murdered
ceanothus hoarding blue
puffballs pyracantha
thorn putting out the eye of a child
everywhere you
look something bearing down arbutus
bottlebrush rhododendron
once in the mountains viburnum we slept under
she says and I remember that time
like a rent in my heart

Minor Fabrications

sometimes I wish
I was a professional scooter or braiser or concrete analyzer
of fragmented evenings
in the moonlight, a caster of lines
maybe
sailer of paper plates
poker of holes
or one whose hands have massaged a heart
or two
calling come on, baby, give,
or something
like that. you can walk around on this earth
carrying a watermelon
or a proviso
detailing the mysteries of the cosmos,
but it's best
to have some professional
experience on your record, a slip
of paper
that says so, and memories
like the taste
of muscadines and mashed potato
sandwiches late at night
in a diner off the highway,
where just now
the cook lies slumped at the coatrack
shot through the heart
by love. nobody wants to be left out
or controlled by vacuous
malingerers

or managers of rerun houses where the stars
try to prepare us
for the worst. even at dam sites
and trails
in reticulated woods after dark
someone is calling for a pro. let us
pick up our instruments
and go. with only a little training
it could be you,
maybe me, handling the stroke, the delve.

THE OTHER LIFE

Close Work

robins show up
not even slightly flabbergasted,
not even
winded, robust no
nonsense characters dispersing from rough gangs,
not wasting time, their bloodstained vests
swollen with tides
of memory.
soon enough we get used
to them. they check into
farm plots and take up space in tiny urban
gardens and scatter into the trees,
go after grubs
and meaty worms unwound
from knots exposed by rain's
housework. scanty violets'
blue buttons
tucked among leaves under the oaks,
a few, over there a clump of crocuses
nodding off.
redbuds, plum trees
in white shawls, green dots
in the elms. gestures and surly approaches,
the yards overrun.
how many times
has this happened. how many
more links
in a silver bracelet dropped in the grass.

Unattainable Goodness

What is it I belong to and find like crushed mint on my shoes,
the stepped rocks presented like a change of heart

that speaks to me as if we are of the same brotherhood,
the casual significance of a bird passing over this field, the way the painter,

with a flick of the brush, made me stop to think first of my father,
then of dying, and how then I was a small boy again,

afraid to make a mistake and alert all the time like the French in Indochina
—what is it I belong to like a residual effect, a remark

dropped handily into the conversation to prove love still exists,
the way—as we went on—the congressman couldn't come up

with an example (that satisfied us) of the soul on lend-lease,
or, in the high valley, how we liked to stay up late, reading the old books

Mother used to keep in the kitchen, until finally Father would come out,
a look in his eyes of a wintering sadness, and tell us to go to bed.

Animal Life

The wind places one hand
on another and breaks off what it was doing to tell a little story

about the interplay of confusion
and solace. I awoke late

and never really made it out of bed.
The usefulness of my preparations

scattered like cicada hulls. I can hear water dripping
behind the walls. The uselessness, did I say that,

of an essential readiness
that prepares us for nothing. I woke up late

and stayed in bed.
The brave orations I wrote,

or was it the numbness I discovered lying
close by, these factors

I never mentioned, or was it the latent
suggestibility I pulled out

like a lariat coiled like a snake,
the sense of shelter, or was it shelter

itself playing along with the last fine phrasing?
It got late early that day.

The water ran out
and we couldn't flush the toilet.

You used to come to the door smiling
so I thought I was in heaven. But this lasted

only a moment. After that,
you said, the bird escaped,

the cabinet broke,
you were dog tired, and hated how we lived.

Clarinet, Sax

split off without a reg sheet
or looseleaf
binder extolling the genuinely terrifying
next moment
I case the house where last night
my two sons and I got into a drunken
fight that sent my
youngest boy to the hospital.
my wife's
already filed for divorce and now
I have to get a room
somewhere else. fine, I say,
that's my style anyway. the trees are enormously
preposterous gold
plumes that hurt the eye
to look at. the mountains, like
soft silk rolled between your fingers,
hang
in a distance
impossible to cross. I take a swim in the Jimpsons'
pool. the water is icy,
jams my breath
into my gut and smells of petroleum.
I'm still a cut above. the limits of possibility
are stacked with the luggage.
I eat a bowl of stew and vomit
it up. my calculations
are awry. sensations
of a clumsy merriment, broken
wind instruments, lie in the grass.

PORTABLE BOATS

One

Some you approach through the woods carrying cakes
Some you sneak up on as if they are orphans
      bandaging the wings of birds
Some you refer to as inconspicuous even though you see them everywhere
Some you place inside your hat and walk around with all day
      as if you are balancing an egg on your head
Some you discover living in the Denver Y
Some you convert to a useless piece of dialogue
Some you fitfully oppose
Some you apply to meekly explaining yourself
      in freakish and ill-favored French
Some you travel to far countries with
Some you misplace
Some you pick the under feathers off of and murmur to fondly
Some you obviously compare to a vanished wilderness
Some you watch dwindle in the rear view mirror
Some you place on the windowsill
Some you embrace without passion
Some you speak to in barrooms and art galleries
      referring to yourself as fraudulent and unfathomable
Some you dispense with lightly
Some you divert into other professions
Some you understand as disguised by moonlight
Some you prepare for a better life
Some you poke
Some you unnerve while dreaming of hotels by the sea
Some you righteously anger
Some you offer pastries to
     and lose sight of frequently

Some you heckle and deride
Some you take casually to your bosom
Some you compare to mice living in granaries
Some you watch from the corner of your eye
Some you badger and push to great acts
Some you dispense with
Some you teach a short solo
Some you love
Some you don't know what to do with
Some you clearly can't speak to without blushing
Some you disturb
Some you compare to a short selection of musical numbers
Some you never get over

Country Churches in Summer

. . . big empty room where dust collects
all week and you can hear the sparrows
in the gallberry scrub the air sheaved with particles
each a world in itself the divisions
that make this shakedown necessary in the first
place settling disparities like a baker's agent sifting flour
through his pale hands the days in summer so long
god gets the idea nothing much goes on in this part of the county
and it takes all the might collected during the week
for the congregation to prove they still
love him best the afterimages of broken harness and love
faltering in the ditch of the heart impressed
and knocked around by hymns that crush
and reconstitute the formal body until the lord climbs off the floor
like a weary fighter sure he can go another round
the universal implementation and ready
proofs a notice for the living remnants in the pews
who huddle as their souls spring upwards like flowers or ponies
and those passing by out on the road hear them
and go on eased by music they didn't realize they'd forgotten.

The Players

I get away among the other players
and practice my style which
includes a section
of close-packed
         moans and a sudden electrified turn
you might not
expect
         if you've never seen it before plus
a look of resolution
that dissolves so quickly
you might think it was
never there
         in the first place. there's a happiness
too you can see
through like a clear plastic
bag
filled with rainwater.
all the others are busy
practicing as well
         and this is one of the good parts.
I watch
and pick up a few pointers
and baldly
universal
techniques that
are a hit everywhere
and I get after them. and you
         too, I say to myself, you too are a hit.

Get Along, Get Along

what I brushed aside went around back
    climbed the fence and got in with its unregulated

placement and dumb alteration
        you could hear the loose

warbling all over the place
    the constant upbraiding and low down

mimicry
    and if it wasn't too much to stand

I would've found out a few things
        but by then I was in a state

bulking up for a run across the border
        which I am deeply grateful for

this slide into a desert situation
    where among the fruit stands and

closely parted evacuation routes you can settle
        beside dry streams and hollows

where little houses keep watch across ransacked valleys
    for the light that is rising somewhere else.

Buying the Fava Beans

. . .scattered about me
        localized and irreverent, careless in manner, the charged bits,
the pressed
and folded collections
        upright and directed in the undramatized parking lot
market where I ask

        about the fava beans
                        among the constant vibration of select billions,
effervescing
and completely
pinpointed like jet planes
silently
angling for fuel,
and the woman, an artist of
particles,
with sleek black hair made of light
and distribution,
                says as she fills

a sack,
        you have to peel them twice, once of the—fuzzy, yellow-green—
outer shell
        and once of the—pale green—skin of the bean
itself, and I turn to the air
breezing lightly against my skin, a looser

gathering of particles
than the lean
and waver, the bluster

about me and about the momentarily
generous being
          who speaks to me, and return,
as from a trip to Ceylon, dusty
and afraid of the night, and I too am part of this,

a collection
          and slowly distributed
assortment—atoning for nothing, owing nothing—like
you—
shifting in the sunlight,
the one
who says it's a little daunting
          to the one who laughs lightly.

After the Wind Died Down

Lush summer
provoked into amplitude, the sense everyone has this year

of a tremendous dosage
just within reach, the boys on silver bikes

off for the big houses set in fields and girls in lemon yellow kerchiefs
trying to stabilize their position

on harmony. We used to walk for miles
just to be together for an hour. Butterbeans

and the muscadines came in at the same time each year.
Sour yellow plums like earbobs

hanging in bushes along the highway. We shaped
our answers to fit the questions, loose

and stirred up almost shining with our own version
of sincerity. You might pedal fifteen miles

for a dance. I say these things
in gratitude, moved by the old blistering

of happiness. The big-bellied trees
take nothing to heart. Day breaks into fragments,

each stamped with the name of a claimant.
Familiar bells ring with the same false solemnity

as always. Traipsing
and pressing our luck we come in off the streets as if from vast unsorted
worlds.

Picture of the Situation

You don't call it pain
you call it daylight
or the rough bark of some oak tree
or the rocks like broken steps at the edge of the woods
but it's not pain
it's not even sadness or anything
you'd set aside or comment on in the diary
you compulsively keep.
Fierce words break through arguments
you get into out in the driveway.
You could set the house
on fire and stand there in the yard still arguing
about how you failed to love her
properly and the fire wouldn't affect you.
Now it's all back in the shed, the
hopes and fabulous way of putting things,
some shed you keep a lock on.
You stand out in the yard
picking the pine sap off the car hood waiting for her
to finish whatever she's
doing inside the house. You light a cigarette
and look at the match
and then you stand there with your head
thrown back. Whatever's pressed up against you
presses so hard breath can't get out. You can't even scream.

By Mechanical Means

Splintery, spring pretends
to stall. Crafted, succinct,
bog hemp & new wild
olive tremble

and appear indistinguishable
from sandspur
and Spanish dagger. Flat
fingers of rain, the care taken

before we set out for supper,
your brother standing a long time gazing
across the pasture
coming up in white clover, a sense

of opportunity missed, swung round
again. The Redeemer, in the body
of a truck gardener, ambles by on his way to the john.
Antinomian heresies

shade toward the barn. Cypresses
shaky in the woods, the proposals of winged
sumac and maidencane taken in stride,
soft landings for briar and crotalaria

bloom. The tiniest is taken
care of. Conventions appraised
and disputes settled. Cow oak and dogwood
seem to push back, extrude

calculated systems of foamy white.
Rambler time. The earnestness
of those who made it through winter
to this spot,

the usual phraseology
and cumbersome mechanics, a child
confessing a childish
crime, a gift carelessly given,

taken back. What's
worked through or failed at
or lost reaches the edge of the barrow
where sorrel

and inkberry thrive, where we loiter,
hunchbacks and enfeebled moralists,
palsied, convulsive, marooned
in this life, willing to talk about it now.